Cottage Crafts

COTTAGE CRAFTS

by
Barbara Ireson

with illustrations by M. J. Mott

FABER AND FABER LIMITED
3 Queen Square London

First published in 1975
by Faber and Faber Limited
3 Queen Square London WC1
Printed in Great Britain by
A. Wheaton & Company Limited Exeter Devon
Filmset by Filmtype Services Limited Scarborough
All rights reserved

ISBN 0 571 10752 4

Contents

I should like to thank everyone who gave me practical help in the preparation of this book and especially Edwina Blackburn who was a constant source of ideas and encouragement.

Introduction

This book is concerned with the accumulated skills and experience developed by generations of country people for creative work in their homes. Its aim is to present a selection of instructions for a wide variety of crafts that need only a few basic tools and the simplest of materials – leaves, flowers, shells, glue, scraps of unwanted cloth, and so on – in order to make many original and pleasing objects. I have deliberately omitted crafts that need special equipment, such as pottery or weaving.

There is today a great revival of interest in these domestic arts which are now being enthusiastically practised throughout the country. For a long time they were a necessary part of a self-sufficient way of life, as were the methods of making cosmetics and materials needed for the cleaning and upkeep of the house.

Some of the things described here need only a few minutes to make; some a few hours; some the evenings of many weeks. I hope that readers in country and town alike will obtain great satisfaction in working with natural and simple materials and will enjoy this glimpse into a way of life that is past.

BARBARA IRESON

11

I · Things that grow

Acorn beads · Garden broom · Cane plant-pot holder · Corn dolly · Dried flowers · Preserving flowers in sand · Lavender bottles · Preserving leaves · Pomanders · Pot pourri · Rush table mats · Teasel mice · Tussie mussies · Wood sculpture · Willow bread basket

ACORN BEADS

Either choose acorns of one size for your necklace, or grade them as you thread them.

You need a strong, sharply-pointed needle and linen thread. If you use the thread double and tie a knot after each acorn, this sets them attractively apart. Dry by hanging them up in a warm room through which a current of air passes.

Acorns make a pleasing necklace, but they will not last indefinitely.

GARDEN BROOM

An ash handle and a thick bundle of slender, pliable twigs make a garden broom that will do a better job of sweeping leaves off lawns and terraces than most brushes.

Cut a 4 foot (120 cm) length of ash that will be comfortable to use as a handle and leave it rough. (If you can't get ash, choose lime or hazel instead.) Try to get a bundle of ling or birch for the head. Remember that ling must be in sap and pliant, so early spring is the best time to cut it.

Begin by cutting a deep nick with a sharp knife in a circle round the handle, about 12 inches (30 cm) from the end that will carry the head. Drill a hole about $\frac{3}{4}$ of an inch (2 cm) across, right through the handle about 2 inches (5 cm) above the nick (this hole used to be

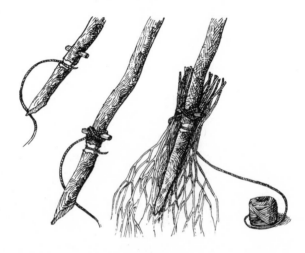

made with a red-hot poker). Whittle a wooden peg to fit so closely into the hole that it has to be hammered in. Allow it to protrude about 1 inch (3 cm) on each side of the handle. Tie one end of a length of tarred-string or strong cord into the nick in the handle, then take enough twigs to make a circle and place them so that they reach up to the wooden peg. Bind the twigs closely to the handle binding the string or cord round the peg as well as round the twigs (this will keep it from slipping or twisting). Take the binding down 12 inches (30 cm) of the broomhead. Encircle the handle with a second layer of twigs and bind upwards ending with a firm twist around the peg. Add a third layer and bind down again. Continue in this way, always binding each time to the peg, until the broom has a good head. It is important to fasten off very securely and this can best be done at the peg.

CANE PLANT-POT HOLDER

A simple article which gives an introduction to canework is a plant-pot holder. To make this you will need a 5-inch (13 cm) round wooden base with 19 holes, 19 number 6 canes 15 inches (39 cm) long, 19 bye-stakes of number 6 canes 11½ inches (25 cm) long and about 2 ounces (56 grammes) of number 3 cane for weaving.

Soak the cane for about ten minutes and then wrap it in a piece of damp towelling or sacking.

Insert a 15 inch (39 cm) cane into each hole of the base so that it protrudes about 3½ inches (9 cm) underneath. Work a foot border with these canes by taking each one in turn and bending it down behind the next cane and in front of the two following ones (work from left to right). Leave the end behind the next cane. When you come to the last three canes, ease up the first three canes worked and

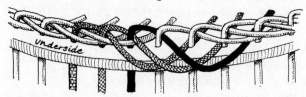

thread the last three underneath them. Each of these ends must go behind one cane and in front of two and finish up on the inside of the border, resting on the wooden base. Pull on the canes from the upper side of the base to tighten the work.

You now continue on the upper side of the base and the canes are referred to as stakes. Four rows of *upsetting* or *waling* are worked

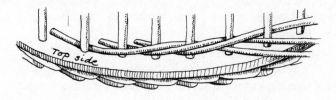

17

to 'set' the stakes in a position equi-distant from each other. Begin by inserting 3 lengths of number 3 cane between the stakes in 3 consecutive spaces. The ends should point inside to the left for about ½ inch (1·25 cm). Weaving begins with the left-hand cane which passes in front of the next two stakes (over the other two working stakes) and behind the third stake, to come out at the front again. Repeat this with the stake which is now on the left and continue in the same way until you reach the starting point and the last-used cane comes out on the left of the first stake.

Take this same cane (it is now the right-hand one of the three) and pass it in front of two stakes and behind one. Take the middle cane in front of two stakes and behind one, and do the same with the one on the left. This finishing process at the end of each row is called 'inverting'.

Begin a new round as at the beginning of the *waling*, working with the left-hand cane of the three. At the end of each round repeat the 'inverting'. Work and finish four rows in this way.

Clip off the left and middle canes so that they are just long enough to pass inside the work under two canes and through to the outside of the basket. Do this first with the middle cane and then with the one on the left.

Now take the bye-stakes and push one down against each stake. It should go down through the upsetting to rest on the base. (This gives you double stakes). The third cane (the one which was not cut off) is now used for *randing*, that is to say, you pass the cane in front of one pair of stakes and behind the next pair. Continue with this simple weave for 2½ inches (6 cm).

When you need to add a new cane leave the end of the old cane resting on the stake inside the basket and insert the new end in the same space beside it, but pointing inwards. Do not add more than one at a time. Instead work with the next cane to be replaced for a few more strokes before inserting another new one.

After $2\frac{1}{2}$ inches (6 cm) of *randing* is complete, insert two new canes on one side of the working cane simply by laying them in. Work four rows of *waling*, remembering the 'inverting' at the end of each one.

Then cut off all three canes starting with the right-hand one, trap them under two canes and bring them through to the outside as before.

Sharpen the ends of the stakes and cut each one to a length that will allow it to pass in front of two stakes to the right, forming a scallop border and down on the outside through the *waling* between the next two stakes. It continues down the outside of the basket and finishes by passing through the lower *waling* to rest on the wooden base. Keep the scallop border even all the way round the basket.

Trim any protruding ends of cane by slicing them off slantwise near the basket and the plant-pot holder is complete.

CORN DOLLY

Dolly has an entirely different meaning here from the one we know commonly. The dictionary shows that it can mean an offering, and this makes sense when you realise that these plaited-corn shapes are part of the harvest ritual to keep the Earth Mother on the land. Even at the beginning of this century farmers in some parts of the country kept a last row of corn standing, or just a last sheaf. They left it in the field until the gleaners went in because their fathers had done this and so had their fathers before them. For the same reason they wove and plaited straw into age-old shapes and hung them on haystacks, in barns and carried them to church for the harvest festival. One common shape was called a 'corn neck' and the Oxford Dictionary defines neck as 'the last handful or sheaf or corn cut at harvest time'. Cornucopias were popular and so was the drop dolly. Some areas favoured particular shapes, and you find corn dolly lanterns and hand bells in Norfolk, umbrellas in Cambridgeshire and riding crops and horseshoes in Suffolk. Today in schools, at evening classes, as well as on some farms, they are still made.

Corn dollies can only be made with hollow straw. Since the type of wheat grown varies throughout the country, if you want to make one it is best to go to a farmer and ask him to sell you an armful of hollow straw with good heads before the combine harvester goes to work on his fields. This much straw will enable you to plait a number of corn dollies. A simple one to begin with and one which takes a good handful only is the drop dolly.

The drop dolly

1. Take five long pieces of straw with good even heads and cut them with sharp scissors just above the first leaf node.

2. Tie them firmly together with raffia just below the heads. Turn the straws upside down. Hold the heads gently but firmly and spread out the straws with your free hand so that they are evenly spaced like the spokes of a wheel. Number the straws from 1 to 5 in an anti-clockwise direction.

3. Starting with straw 1, bend it across 2 and 3 to place it between 3 and 4. Move the straws in your hand a quarter turn clockwise.

4. Straw 3 is then bent across 1 and 4. Lay straw 4 across 3 and 5. Lay straw 5 across 4 and 2. Keep moving the straws in a clockwise direction as you work.

5. Bend straw 2 across 5 so that it lies parallel to 1.

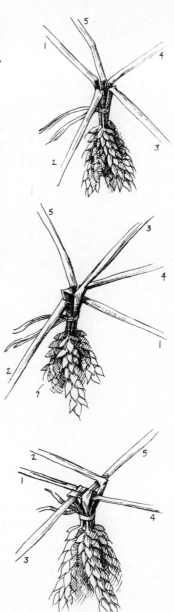

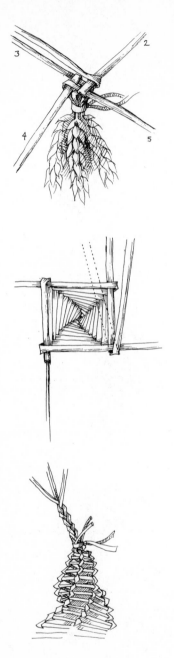

6. Bend straw 1 over 2 to lie parallel with 3.

7. Straw 3 then goes under and over 1 to lie parallel with 4.

8. Continue this way bending each straw over the next two and moving the second up and over in the same way. Keep turning your corn dolly as you work.

9. Whenever you come towards the end of a weaver straw, cut it off at a corner of the weave and push the thin end of a new straw into the centre of the old one. (It goes in more easily if you snip it slantwise with your scissors first.)

10. While you continue in this way, laying the moving straw parallel to the straw two beyond it, the dolly will widen. When it is about half as long as you want it to be, begin to overlap the moving straw. This will gradually decrease the width.

11. To finish off you will need to be working with three straws at least 8 inches long (20 cm), so add new weavers if it is necessary. Bend the straws upwards and tie them firmly with raffia. Plait the three longest straws and bend them round to make a loop. Tie the loop with raffia to the two other straws close to the end of the weaving.

12. Tie a bow with ribbon just above the corn heads and hang the drop corn dolly from its loop.

22

It's a good idea to dry flowers throughout the blooming season and store them for use in the winter. Love-lies-bleeding, pearly ever-lasting, lavender, larkspur, lupins, monbretia, salvias, spirea and hydrangeas are all flowers that dry well, and there are many others besides.

Pick the flowers on a dry day and choose only the ones that are not yet in full bloom. Begin the drying process immediately, before

the flowers have time to wilt. This is done by stripping off all the leaves and tying about four or five stems loosely together so that mildew will not form between them. They need to be somewhere dry but also where there is a current of air, so a shed or attic with an open window is a good place. Put up a clothes line or a length of strong string and tie the bunches individually along it. Suspend large flowers singly.

When the flowers feel dry to the touch stand them upright in a pot or tray of sand to allow the florets to fall back to their natural position. The petals can then be gently smoothed out at this stage and left to dry completely.

If the flowers are to be displayed immediately, stand them in containers with no water; if they are to be stored, handle them carefully and put them in a cardboard box, making sure that the blooms are not pressed too closely together.

PRESERVING FLOWERS IN SAND

If you have a steady hand you can preserve flowers by using sand, which helps them to keep their colour and shape for a long time.

Place a lump of clay or a piece of plasticine in the bottom of a jar tall enough to take the flowers. Stick the stalks in the clay so that the flowers can stand upright and then slowly and very gently pour in enough fine, dry sand to cover them completely. Keep the jar in a warm place where no damp can get to it and leave it there for about three weeks. Pour out the sand with great care and the flowers are ready for use in a dry pot.

LAVENDER BOTTLES

Old English lavender (*lavendula officinalis*) is the best kind for making lavender bottles. Pick your lavender just before you are ready to begin the bottles and choose stalks of flowers that are just opening. You will need about twenty-two heads with long sturdy stalks. Tie them together with a piece of wool just below the heads, then bend the stalks back over the heads to form a bottle-shape. Leave enough of a $1\frac{1}{2}$ yard (135 cm) long piece of narrow ribbon at the neck of the bottle to make a half bow, and draw the ribbon down through the inside to begin weaving from the base with the other end. You weave by going under and over every two stalks, pulling the ribbon firmly as you go, and continuing round and round to

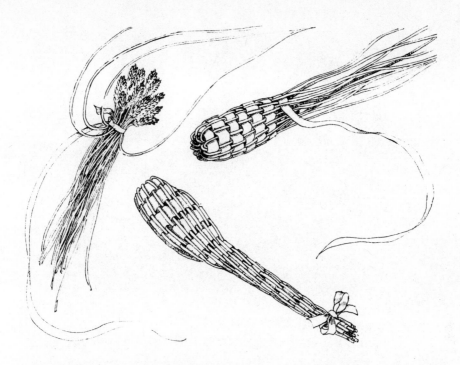

the top. Enough of the ribbon should remain to make the bow with the end that was left there. Cut the protruding ends of the stalks so that they are neat and even and the bottle is ready to go into your cupboards and drawers. Its fragrance is given off whenever it is pressed and a lavender bottle lasts for months.

PRESERVING LEAVES

One way of preserving leaves is by pressing them between several layers of newspaper. Spread out the sprays of leaves between layers of newspaper so that none overlap with others. Put them under a weighty mat or under heavy books. Leave them there undisturbed for several weeks.

Ferns and beech leaves look particularly attractive when they have been preserved in this way, but be sure to choose sprays that have not begun to shrivel.

Leaves can also be preserved by standing them for about three weeks in a solution of glycerine and water. This solution is made by adding boiling water to glycerine in the proportion of two-thirds to one-third. Make the solution in a large jug, or perhaps a baby's bath, or a bucket for tall sprays; then scrape the stems of the branches, crush the ends with a rolling pin or a hammer and immerse them entirely. As the solution evaporates during the following week or so, top it up. At the end of three weeks the leaves will be a deep brown. Beech, forsythia and laurel are subjects that look particularly well after this treatment.

Whichever method you use, don't forget that the preserved leaves should be placed in pots with no water.

The word pomander was evolved, possibly in mediaeval times, to describe an apple – pome – carrying fragrant spices fixed with ambergris – ambre. It was believed that they could ward off infection as well as sweeten the air, for at that time the absence of drainage and sanitation meant that houses and streets were full of unpleasant odours. Wealthy Elizabethans carried their perfumed herbs and spices in pomanders worked in filagree gold, silver, or ivory: a collection of these can be seen at the Victoria and Albert Museum. Since that time people have continued to make pomanders because of their long-lasting quality and their delicate perfume and the one which is most common today has an orange as its base.

It is simple to make and you just need an orange with a thin skin, ½ ounce (14 grammes) of cloves and 1 ounce (28 grammes) each of ground orris root and cinnamon. Your only tool is a slender knitting needle, and you can buy narrow ribbon, coloured-headed pins, sequins or beads as you wish, for decoration.

Begin by sticking two circles of narrow adhesive tape round the orange at right angles to each other. With the knitting needle, pierce the skin between the tapes with close holes. Push a clove

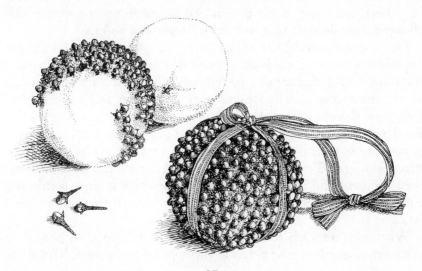

stalk into every hole. Tip the ground orris root and the cinnamon into a plastic bag and shake up the orange in it. Take out the orange, wrap it in tissue paper and leave it for about five weeks in an airing cupboard.

When you remove it, the pomander will be dry and will not moulder. Take off the adhesive tape and tie the narrow ribbon round the channels left across the skin. Use pins with coloured heads to keep the ribbon in place.

If you want to make a number of pomanders to place in a bowl, prick the skins all over with holes and do not bother to make channels with tape.

It's worth experimenting over the making of pomanders. Try using a lemon instead of an orange, and, before putting it in the airing cupboard, sprinkle it with musk or flower oil or even scent. The decoration can be quite an art too. By attaching beads and sequins you can make your pomander look quite exotic and richly ornamented.

POT POURRI

For centuries rose petals and those of other heavily scented flowers have been made into a pot pourri and placed in open bowls which allowed their delicate fragrance to perfume our rooms.

One of the attractions of making pot pourri is that you can experiment with all kinds of scented flowers and create your own fragrance. Old fashioned, heavily-scented roses are a popular ingredient and so are thyme, rosemary, lavender and lemon balm. Pick your flowers before they are fully in bloom on a dry day when the dew has gone. Detach the petals and put them on strong brown paper, or on several sheets of newspaper in a dry place away from strong sunlight. Turn them twice a day. After a while they will lose their moisture and become brittle. If you are storing them while you collect other flowers throughout the summer put them in a closed box.

When you are ready to make your pot pourri, a good combination is six times as many rose petals as those of other flowers. Mix them

together in a large bowl and add one tablespoon (28 grammes) of powdered orris root to fix the scent and another tablespoon of mixed spices like clove, allspice, nutmeg and cinnamon. Other fragrant ingredients such as dried orange and lemon peel, ground tonquin beans and sandalwood are worth adding. Just a few drops of essential flower oils will further enhance the fragrance.

The pot pourri can now be put out in bowls to give off its scent, but should you be storing it, be sure to put it in air-tight containers.

RUSH TABLE MATS

If there is marshy land, or a pond or lake near you, there will probably be some *juncus effusus*, Britain's most common rush, that you can gather. Cut the rushes as close as possible to the roots and tie them into bundles. Dry the rushes upright where the wind can blow through them and keep them away from strong light.

Whether you have dried your own rushes, or bought them, you will have to dampen them again before beginning to weave. Lay them flat on grass and pour water on them from a watering can. Keep turning them so that they are evenly dampened. Let the water drain off and then roll them in a damp towel or a piece of damp hessian. You can use them after about four hours.

Choose ten rushes about $\frac{1}{4}$ inch ($\frac{1}{2}$ cm) in diameter for the weavers, and cut ten more of $\frac{1}{2}$ inch (1 cm) diameter in 16 inch (36 cm) lengths for the stakes.

The centre of the mat is woven with the stakes in check weave or single weave. This is under one and over one with flattened rushes.

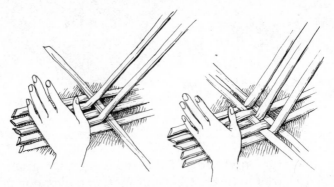

Lay five stakes next to each other in a row. Put your left hand down at right angles to the stakes. The length of stake in front of the palm of your hand should be just more than half. Lift the 2nd

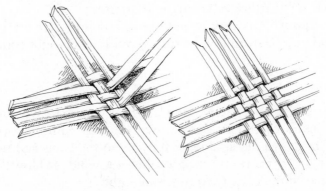

and 4th stake and slide a new stake across. Lay them down and lift the 1st, 3rd and 5th stake and slide another stake across. Flatten those three stakes and continue check weave until all ten stakes are incorporated.

Bend one of the finer rushes in half and loop it behind the first stake. The ends are two weavers. Mark them 1 and 2 with a ball-point pen. With these two rushes, you continue in pairing weave:

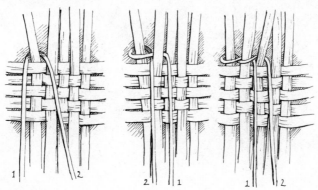

1 passes over 2 in front of the first stake and goes behind the second stake. Then 2 passes over 1 in front of the second stake and behind the third stake. Continue like this using the weavers alternately. Make sure that you keep the stakes evenly spaced.

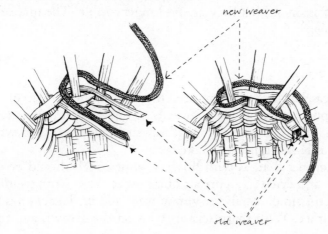

new weaver

old weaver

31

Whenever a weaver gets short, add the thin end of a new one and work double for three or four weaves.

Continue in this pairing weave until the mat is about 8 inches in diameter (you can make it smaller or bigger if you wish). Using a football lacing awl, thread the weaving ends in turn through the eye and draw them down through four rounds of pairing weave.

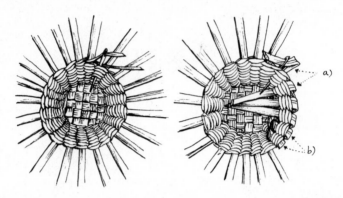

Dampen the stakes before beginning the border. Push the eye of the awl up through the last four rounds of pairing to the edge of the mat close to a stake. Thread the stake through the eye and draw it down the pairing weave. Repeat this with each stake.

Trim the stakes and the weavers close to the mat with a very sharp pair of scissors so that they are no longer visible. The mat should be reversible.

TEASEL MICE

Dried teasel heads have long been used for raising the nap of woollen cloth and in flower arrangements. They can also be made into families of amusing small creatures such as teasel mice which are very simple and quick to make.

Remember that, as with flowers, your teasels should be cut on a dry day and dried in a current of air away from strong sunlight.

Take the small teasels for young mice and the larger ones for full-grown mice. With sharp scissors trim off the growth and the stalks from the teasel and snip off an area of prickles from each one to allow it to sit squatly. Give each mouse two eyes by forcing cloves on stalks into the teasel, and two ears and two feet by forcing in pieces of fir cone. Make a hole with a knitting needle and push a string tail into it. (A dab of clear glue will ensure that all these stay in place.)

Try making another creature using a small teasel with a large one to make a head and a body. Give it stick legs and large leaf ears. A variety of effects can be achieved with simple things from the fields and woods.

TUSSIE MUSSIES

Tussies mussies were carried, as were nosegays and pomanders, for their fragrance and for the protection it was thought they gave from infection. A fifteenth-century English/Latin dictionary mentions them.

The Victorians attributed a symbolic language of love to flowers, so each tussie mussie, with its own combination of flowers and herbs, could carry a personal amorous message. It also carried a perfume that depended on the skill of the tussie mussie maker in mixing the pungent herbs and fragrant flowers.

33

Start your tussie mussie with a handsome single flower. This is the centre piece. The other flowers, leaves and herbs are now arranged in concentric circles around it. Keep each circle in place with wool as you complete it. The tussie mussie can be as large or as small as you wish it to be, but tie off the wool securely when it is finished. It is prettily set off by poking the stems through a lace-patterned paper doily and twisting silver foil round them.

WOOD SCULPTURE

Pieces of wood in shapes suitable for wood sculpture turn up all over the place. Keep your eyes open in the garden, in the country and on the shore. The gnarled and twisted pieces are what you want. Heavy tormented-looking old roots are particularly suitable.

Leave your wood in a dry place for a couple of weeks, then strip off the bark and, after looking very carefully at the shape, remove all unpleasing protuberances. Smooth the surfaces first with a coarse sandpaper, then with a fine one. Do not hurry this process. When the

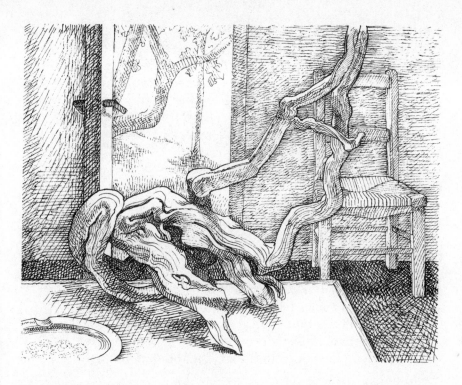

shape and the texture of the sculpture is as you want it, rub in bees-wax polish. Whether you simply nourish the wood or polish it is a matter of personal taste.

A wood sculpture is best glued to a thin wooden base. It will then stand firmly and be displayed to advantage. It can also be used in flower arrangements.

WILLOW BREAD BASKET

The inter-weaving of twigs, rushes, leaves, and other things that grow is one of the oldest crafts. Scholars have found evidence that for over 9000 years man has used basketry to make himself houses (including the walls, doors and roofs), simple boats and rafts, furniture, fish traps, and many other necessities. The North American Indian moulded pots in baskets; pottery found at Ur in Mesopotamia

35

bears the impression of coiled basketry too. The Romans made basketry furniture, cradles, light carriages and even chariots. The Greeks made wicker travelling baskets. Merchants and traders needed baskets. Shapes evolved in accordance with their needs and some of these have changed little over the centuries. The machine cannot make as good a basket as a pair of skilled hands and workshops where baskets for the farmer and the fisherman are hand woven can still be found.

To make a bread basket it is best to use brown or white willow rods cut during the winter and stored. Handicraft stores that do not themselves supply willow will probably be able to tell you where to write for it. Most British willow comes from Somerset where the rich moorland drained by the Parret, Yeo and Tone is particularly well suited to its growth.

Before you can begin work with willow, it has to be soaked so that it becomes pliable. White rods will be all right after an overnight soaking, but you may have to soak brown rods for several days. Drain them on their butt ends away from strong sunlight and wind and then roll them in wet sacking. They will be ready after an hour or so, but only take out from the sacking the rods you need to work with.

Work at a table and have handy a pair of secateurs, a sharp knife, a bodkin and a pair of round-nosed pliers.

1. Choose 6 willows rods of similar thickness and colour and cut them down to 12 inches (30 cm). Lay them in threes to form a cross.
2. Double a long rod and holding the cross in your left hand, loop it behind the top three rods. You now have a pair of weavers.

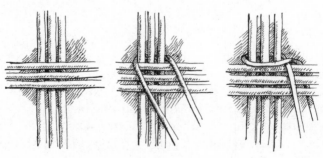

3. Twist the left weaver over the right weaver and bend it closely behind the right arm of the cross.

4. Turn the cross in your hand so that the right arm becomes the top arm. Twist the new left-hand weaver over the right weaver and bend it closely down behind the new right arm of the cross as before.

5. This weave is called pairing. Continue like this for two rounds, turning the cross to the left for each new step.

6. Spread out the 12 rods of the cross like the spoke of a wheel. Make sure they are evenly spaced out and then, bending them slightly upwards, continue in pairing weave, this time round each rod.

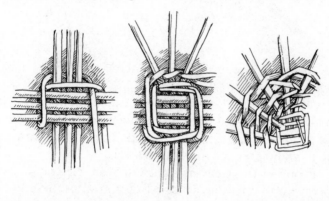

7. You can make the base of the basket just as big as you like. New weavers can be added by pushing in an end which has been sharpened with a knife just behind the old rod. Force it well down.

8. When you are ready to begin the sides, trim the rods of the cross, but make sure that you have two weavers of a good length.

9. Now you need to take 24 new rods of similar thickness and colour from the sacking. Cut them down to 12 inches (30 cm) with your knife. See over for diagram.

10. Sharpen them and push them into the basket bottom, one on each side of the original stakes of the cross. They need to penetrate about $2\frac{1}{2}$ inches (6 cm).

11. Lay the base flat on the table and bend up the new stakes at right angles. Tie them at the top to keep them in position.

12. Now you need a third weaver. Sharpen the end and push it into

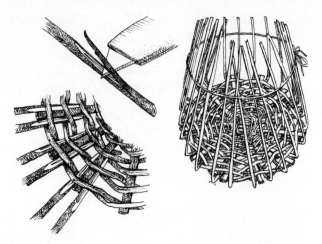

the space between the upright rods which come after the two original weavers.

13. The weave for beginning the sides is called waling. Take weaver A in front of the next two uprights and behind the third bringing it in front of the fourth. Do this with weaver B and then with weaver C. Continue in waling weave for three rounds.

14. Cut off one of the weavers slantwise near the tray and resume pairing weave until the sides are as tall as you want them to be. Add new weavers when necessary as before.

15. To finish, cut off your two weavers slantwise and push them down as closely as you can to an upright rod.

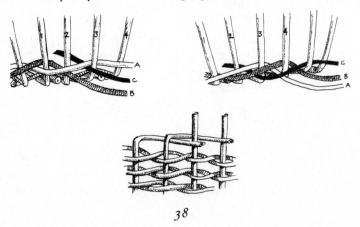

16. Make a border by bending the end of each upright in turn behind the one to the right of it and bring it up in front of the one after. Trim it off neatly.

2 · Making pictures

Brass rubbings · Decorated eggs · Feather pictures · Pressed flower pictures · Skeleton leaves · Potato printing · Seaweed pictures · Seed pictures · Shell work

A brass rubbing is not just a decorative wall hanging or picture; it's a record of the appearance of someone who lived centuries ago. Incised in brass are armour, clothes, head-dresses, children and even pets, all there for us to see.

The Victoria and Albert Museum have published a catalogue of brasses in British churches. There are over four thousand and some of

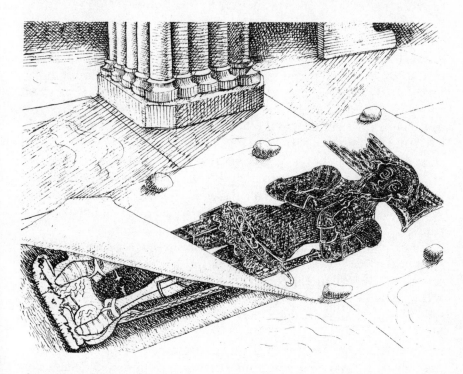

them date from as early as 1300. This catalogue is available through bookshops.

Permission to make a rubbing of a brass can be obtained from the vicar or verger of the church. Charges vary, but £1 is an average fee. It is wise to make your appointment to do the rubbing when you are least likely to interfere with people who come to the church to worship.

Buy architects' paper, black heel ball, acorn crayons and a plastic eraser from an art shop if you want to make a black rubbing on white paper. If you want a more spectacular rubbing, buy gold or silver heel ball and rub on to black, dark blue or brown paper. Whatever kind of rubbing you decide to make, you will need a roll of masking tape from a decorator's shop.

Take a soft brush with you and dust off the brass you have chosen to work on, making sure to remove as much dust as you can from the incising. Study the brass and make a few notes about its detail. Cut your paper larger than the brass – at the top and bottom it should be at least 12 inches (30 cm) longer. Stick it with masking tape to the stone surround (it must stay like this until the rubbing is finished). Run your fingers round the edge of the brass to give an indication of the outlines, then holding your paper firmly in place with one hand, grip the heel ball in the palm of your other hand and begin to rub over the brass with short hard strokes. Start at an edge, but try never to go over the edges. Rub in all directions as you work over the brass to avoid strokes showing. Dust off loose bits of heel ball that fall on to the paper as you work. Read the notes you made and try to make sure that every detail of the brass is well rubbed.

Be careful not to tear your paper on brass rivets or on damaged areas of the brass. When the rubbing is finished, remove the masking tape carefully, roll up the paper and slip it into a cardboard tube. The acorn crayons are for touching up at home and the plastic eraser is for light heel ball marks that may have strayed over the edge of the brass.

Brass rubbings hang well if glued at either end round wooden dowelling. It's worth giving some attention to finding a decorative piece of cord to hang them by. Coloured woollen curtain ties can look very fine.

DECORATED EGGS

Wrap white-shelled eggs closely in the brown outer skins of onions (a light gauze will keep the skins in place). Boil the eggs and when they are cooked the shells will be found to be mottled in attractive shades of yellow.

If you want to paint eggs and use them for display, you must begin by blowing them. Make a small hole at one end of each egg and a slightly larger hole at the other end. Blow through the small hole until the shell is empty.

Draw patterns on the shells; masking tape, sellotape and stencils can all be used to get a professional finish. For instance, cut out leaf

and flower shapes from masking tape and stick them on a shell. Paint all round the tape with a background colour. When this is dry, take off the shapes and paint in the flowers and leaves. Rectangular patterns and ribbons of colour can be achieved by using sellotape in the same way. If you use a stencil, paint your design first and fill in the background when it is dry. It's best to give egg shells a coat of clear varnish after using water colours, but this isn't necessary with either acrylic or enamel paints.

A bowl of egg shells, all painted with different patterns in different colours, looks extremely decorative. Painted egg shells can also be strung up on coloured linen thread.

FEATHER PICTURES

If you ask at the right season, butchers and poulterers will very often have attractive and colourful feathers to give you. Look in the countryside near ponds and pools and you will find unusual feathers to add to your collection. Feathers get caught in hedges and bushes,

so if you search about you can soon get the variety in size and colour that you need for a picture.

When you are ready to begin, buy a piece of insulating board the right size for your picture and some clear strong glue and a spatula. You can colour your board by painting it with matt emulsion paint, or glue on silk or hessian or some other material that pleases you. A pair of tweezers is a great help and so is a small soft-haired painting brush.

Your picture should be drawn first on paper and then on the board. It may be representational or it may be a pattern. Sometimes seeds, dried flowers, sequins or beads can be used along with feathers to give an impression of richness. Only begin to use the glue when you know where your material is going. Work over a small section of your drawing at a time. Spread the glue thinly and then, with the tweezers, put your subjects in place one by one. Use the paint brush to spread out the feathers so that they lie naturally on the board.

When your picture is complete, set it aside and leave it undisturbed overnight. If you hope to keep it for a long time, it is worth putting it under glass in a frame.

PRESSED FLOWER PICTURES

Gather the flowers for your picture on a dry day after the dew has gone. Bear in mind the design you want to make and the colour harmonies or contrasts of the flowers as you make your choice. Leaves enhance the picture if they have an interesting shape and are delicately formed.

Once they are cut, the flowers and leaves go between sheets of blotting paper. Spread them out well so that they do not touch each other. Large and complicated flowers need to have their petals pressed separately. This means the flower has to be reassembled later on. If you are beginning this art, it is wisest to choose simple flowers, for the effect you can get with them is extremely beautiful. Never try to press thick stalks, they will only look ugly. Press plenty of delicate well-shaped ones.

When both sheets of blotting paper are in place, carefully lift them with the flowers in between and lay them on several newspapers. Put several more on top. Heavy books on top of all this will do the pressing. The flowers should be undisturbed for about four weeks.

Preparing the frame

Old frames often set off flower arrangements well. Find one complete with its glass if you can. Cut a piece of strong cardboard to fit the frame and glue a covering of hessian or another material of similar texture on to it. Make certain the glue is dry and the material is well stuck down before you begin mounting your flowers.

47

Mounting

When the flowers are pressed, experiment carefully on a board to find an arrangement that pleases you. Use a clear glue that is suitable for fabrics and put just a dab on each flower as you press it into place. Leaves and stalks may need a little glue in several places. When the picture is complete lay a sheet of strong brown paper over it and

gently go all over the picture, pressing everything down. Then remove the paper and leave the picture to dry. The next day you can put the glass in the frame, the picture behind it and last of all a wooden or board backing. Seal the gap between the frame and the backing with strips of sticky brown paper. This keeps out damp and dust.

Your picture is now ready for hanging.

Skeleton leaves make unusual and delicate pictures and greetings cards. They are decorative on their own, but they can also be used with pressed flowers.

The fleshy part of the leaf has to be decayed before it will part from its skeleton. Cover leaves with rainwater, place them outside in an

open container and leave them there until the flesh begins to rot. Keep topping up the water as it evaporates.

You then take them out and put them on a flat white plate. Pour clean water on them. The white plate shows up the leaf skeleton clearly and a soft-haired brush will ease away the decaying tissue. When the skeletons are detached, wash them and pat them dry with a soft cloth before putting them between blotting paper under a pad of newspapers and some heavy books.

It's quite simple to bleach skeleton leaves. Just soak them for a few hours in a dilute solution of bleach (an eggcupful of bleach to a gallon of water) and when you take them out, wash them and dry them again. After bleaching they can also be coloured with vegetable dyes but then, of course, they have to be dried once more.

Mount your leaves on card or on board covered with fabric in the same way as is suggested for pressed flowers.

POTATO PRINTING

For this you need a potato, a sharp knife, powder paints mixed in saucers and drawing paper. Cover your working surface with a thick pad of newspaper and begin by cutting a chunk of potato that you can hold comfortably in your hand. First make a design on a piece of rough paper, then cut away at the flat surface of the potato until only the raised pattern is left.

Spread out the drawing paper and dip the raised part of the potato into one of the colours. Shake it to remove excess paint and begin to print in the top left-hand corner. Work across the paper.

Even a simple pattern can be used to build up more complicated designs and by changing colours the attractiveness of the print is further increased. It is important to wipe the potato clean between colours.

If simple objects like flowers, leaves, trees, animals and birds are cut on separate potatoes, pictures can be built up. Houses or churches should have roofs or spires printed individually.

Potato prints are a good way of producing your own Christmas or birthday cards.

SEAWEED PICTURES

Seaweeds vary greatly in shape, colour and texture so it's a good idea to collect them in different places. Dry and store them until you have as many as you need.

Each time you bring home seaweed wash it in salt water and dry it gently with a cloth. Then put it between large sheets of blotting paper making sure that the fronds don't overlap. Put the blotting paper between layers of newspaper and press under heavy books. After about a week the seaweed is flat and dry and ready either to be used or to be stored.

It's worth experimenting to find the right surface for mounting your seaweed. Hessian on board looks attractive; wood rubbed

over with oil is also suitable. The mounting and arranging calls for imagination, and this is where you have your chance to make an original and interesting picture. When your board is ready, experiment by trying the seaweed in different positions. Try always to make it look natural in the way it lies. When you are ready to fix it in position, use a clear glue sparingly so that you do not spoil your mount.

A seaweed picture looks well under an unframed sheet of glass fixed with metal clips to the mount.

Another type of seaweed picture

If you want to try another method, take a frame with a back to it and spread a thin layer of wet cement inside the frame. Then press shells and pebbles and seaweed into the cement and leave it to dry, thus making an original relief picture. Remember that it is well worth sketching a rough design before beginning to set any materials into the cement.

Look around grocers, pet shops, continental food shops and agricultural suppliers, and you will find that the variety in the colour, shape and texture of common seeds on sale is so great that it is difficult to make a choice for a seed picture. Think of pumpkin seeds, coffee beans, chick peas, lentils, butter beans, rice, Indian corn, canary seed, mustard seed, apple pips and orange pips and immediately you see how attractive they could all be in building up a design or picture. Sketch a rough plan on paper, thinking what colours and shapes would suit it best, and then transfer it carefully onto a piece of insulating board the size you want your picture to be.

You will need a strong glue like Dufix or Evo-stik Resin. Put a coating on the board where you intend to begin, but only work on a small area at a time. Some seeds you can place on the board individually; some are too small and have to be shaken on with great

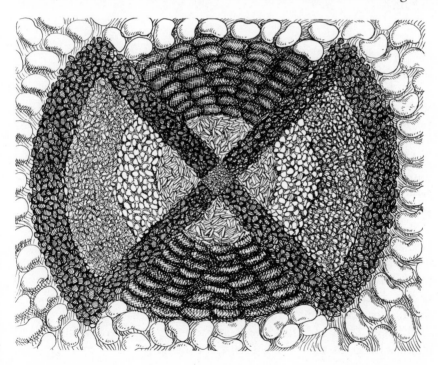

care. A pair of tweezers helps in guiding seeds where you want them to go and a wooden skewer with a dab of glue on the end is helpful for picking them up.

Leave the picture undisturbed overnight so that the glue has time to set properly. When you move it a few seeds may fall off, but it will not take long to put them back where they belong. Once everything is dry, it's quite a good idea to give the seeds a coat of polyurethane varnish. This helps them to keep their colour and protects them from damp and dust.

Give careful attention to the mounting of your picture – a natural substance looks best. Wood enhances the colours of the seeds, and a cork or hessian-covered board can look very well too. Glue your picture to the mount, which should be about 4 inches (10 cm) larger all the way round. When the glue has set, screw a couple of ring hooks into the back of your mounting board and it is ready to hang.

SHELL WORK

It's worth collecting shells whenever you have the chance for there are all kinds of things you can do with them. Wash them to get rid of any sand that still clings to them and dry well.

One of the most obvious ways of using shells is gluing them on to something you wish to decorate. Boxes, lamps, paper-weights, plant-pots are just a few of the things that can be made more attractive with shells. If an object is not beautiful to begin with, shells will do little for it, so do remember to choose things that are pleasing to the eye. To deepen the colour of your shells and give them a sea-wet look, coat them with clear varnish and leave them to dry. When you are ready to begin decorating something, try various arrangements of shells first. They usually look better if they are spaced out, but small boxes look well entirely covered in shells. Spread the edge of the shells lightly with china cement and once the decoration is finished, put the object away for the required time to set.

Crushed shell can look most attractive particularly when glued to the surface of shiny tins. The small pieces protrude at angles and reflect the light. Put your glue on to a small area at a time and sprinkle the crushed shell on to it.

Shells can also be used in a number of ways to make pictures. Crushed shells can be used to create mosaic designs. Whole shells can be arranged in patterns, or to make a picture. It is always worth sketching out your design on paper first for this allows you to work quickly once the glue is applied.

A very different kind of picture can be made by spreading the backing of a picture frame with a thin layer of wet cement. Seaweed and pebbles can be used with shells in this kind of picture to give variety in texture, shape and colour.

3 · Needle and thread

*Peg dolls · Pipe-cleaner doll · Woollen dolls · French knitting ·
Hobby horse · Lavender scent bags · Patchwork · Scented pillows ·
Rag rug · Crocheted rag rugs · Samplers · Smocking*

Two clothes-pegs, the top of a toothpaste tube and some non-toxic paint are all you need to make a toy soldier. With a small hand-saw or coping saw cut off the prongs from one peg. These will make arms. Sandpaper them and the remaining peg, and then knock in two very strong but thin nails to attach the arms to the body. Make

certain that the paint you are going to use is safe for children's toys and then paint a smart uniform on the soldier. A dab of glue will keep his hat on his head and you can paint him a face.

If you want a girl-doll, make a dress with some oddments in a gay cotton material and glue wool on her head to make hair. A little cotton bonnet to match the dress completes the doll.

Four pipe cleaners and a $\frac{1}{2}$ inch (1·25 cm) slice from a cork are the basic materials needed to make this doll.

Make the first pipe cleaner into a circle by twisting the two ends together. Part of this circle fits round the head and the rest forms the basis for the body. Slip a second pipe cleaner through just under the head to form arms and twist it round a couple of times to ensure that

it is firmly secured. A third cleaner goes through the bottom of the loop for the legs. Now tightly twist the loop so that the arms and legs cannot slip out and bend the ends to make hands and feet. Bind the last cleaner round and round the body to make it less spindly and to give it bulk. A circle of linen-faced adhesive tape will stick onto the cork so that you can draw a face or stick on features made out of scraps of felt. Strands of wool make the hair. Your doll can be attractively dressed with odd pieces of woollen or cotton materials.

Children love making these malleable little dolls look as though they are dancing, running, hopping or crawling. With a little imagination you can create ballet dancers, witches on broomsticks, sailors dancing a hornpipe, soldiers drilling, and any number of other characters.

The diagram shows a very simple rag doll. Adapt this pattern to the size you want and allow a $\frac{1}{2}$ inch (about 1·5 cm) for seams. Cut it out twice on double material and you have the back and front of the doll straightaway. Stitch all round the doll with strong cotton, but leave 4 inches (10 cm) open down one side. Fill the doll through this open area with plastic foam chips or with finely cut pieces of nylon stocking. Use the handle of a wooden spoon to push stuffing into the arms and legs. Do not squash it down. The filling should be

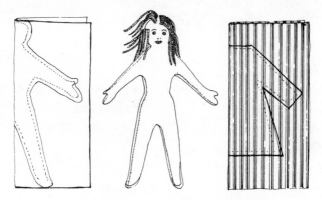

firm and even, so that the doll does not look lumpy. When the doll is ready, sew up the opening with small, neat stitches.

Never make eyes with buttons. They are too easily swallowed by infants. A handicraft shop will sell you small pieces of felt from which you can cut out eyes and a mouth. Stick them on with fabric glue. Stitched brown eyebrows look well. Cut lengths of wool for hair and stitch them on firmly at a centre parting. If you want longer, thicker hair, stitch more lengths farther down the head as shown. Trim to get the effect you want.

The easiest kind of dress to make is one which, like the doll, can

be cut out from a single pattern. Double your material for cutting out. It is also very adaptable, since when lengthened it makes a long dress or nightdress. Gingham cotton prints look particularly attractive on rag dolls.

WOOLLEN DOLLS

Woollen dolls are made by winding and tying. Cut a strip of cardboard about 5 inches long. Wind your wool round this once and make it fast with a knot. Keep on winding until you have gone round another thirty times then slip it off the cardboard. Do not break off your wool; tie it tightly around the loops about a $\frac{1}{2}$ inch (1·25 cm) from the top. Fasten off neatly at that point and then bind it round the loops again about 1 inch (2·5 cm) further down. Cut through the top $\frac{1}{2}$ inch (1·25 cm) loops to make the hair. The face is the inch (2·5 cm) beneath.

Now cut another strip of carboard large enough to make the two

arms. Wind the wool around this about fourteen times and fasten by tying. This is then slipped off the cardboard. Holding it firmly in its loops, slip it through the centre of the body. Tie round the body under the arms and again about $1\frac{1}{2}$ inches (3·75 cm) down to give the doll a body. Divide the underneath loops in two, so that the doll now has legs. A tight twist of wool at the end of the arms and legs makes hands and feet. Double two pipe cleaners and insert one into the doll's arms. Push the other one into the body just under the neck: one half goes into the right leg, the other half into the left leg. These pipe cleaners are not seen and give strength and flexibility.

Embroider a face with coloured wools and the doll is complete.

FRENCH KNITTING

Knock four small nails firmly into the top of a wooden cotton reel. Space them evenly round the hole. About half an inch of the nails needs to be standing above the reel. See over for diagrams.

Thread the end of your wool down through the centre of the reel and out of the other end. Hold it securely. Now wind the wool from the ball twice round the first nail. Lift the lower strand of wool over the top strand and over the nail with a blunt bodkin or a slender wooden cocktail stick. Do this with the next three nails. Next time round pass your wool round the outside of the nails and lift each

stitch over the wool. Continue like this and before long a knitted tube will come out from the bottom hole of the cotton reel. Keep working and pulling out the knitting as it grows.

French knitting grows quite quickly, and the length you knit will depend on what you are going to make. You can stitch it round and round, shaping it as you go to make hats or tea cosies. If you keep it flat as you stitch, you can make mats for the bedroom or bathroom. Rainbow wool gives a very gay effect when used for French knitting.

HOBBY HORSE

A broomstick, a brown woollen sock, cotton wool, a few strong tacks, some black wool, felt scraps, a needle and a castor will make a hobby horse. Begin by stuffing the sock with cotton wool. Force the broomstick up into the back of the heel. With two felt circles glued in position for the eyes, and a little skill with the needle to sew a mouth and nostrils with the black wool, the toe of the sock becomes

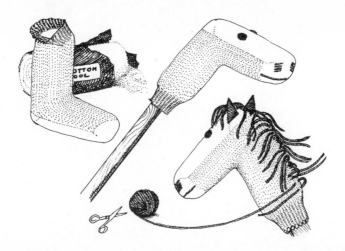

the hobby horse's face. Hammer in a circle of brass drawing-pins or tacks round the neck in order to keep the broomstick firmly in position. Small triangles of leather can be sewn on to make alert-looking ears. The mane is made by looping pieces of black wool

65

12 inches (30 cm) long through the back of the neck. Pull both ends of each piece of wool through the loop tightly. Give the hobby horse a thick mane and arrange some shorter bits between its eyes. With colourless glue, fix coloured tape or braid in a circle just above the nose and another just below the ears to represent the bridle. Another strip goes from the first circle, up one side of the head, round the back of the neck and down the other side of the head. Decorate the joins with circles of coloured felt. Screw the castor into the base of the broomstick and the hobby horse is complete.

LAVENDER SCENT BAGS

If possible, choose old fashioned lavender (*lavendula officinalis*) for your scent bags. Pick sprigs which are not quite fully in bloom on a dry day after the dew has gone. Gather some mint and thyme too. Dry them all on strong brown paper or several sheets of newspaper

away from damp and from strong sunlight (an airing cupboard is a good place). Leave them there until they are brittle.

Put your lavender and herbs into a bowl; a good proportion is 4 oz (112 grammes) of lavender flowers to $\frac{1}{2}$ oz (14 grammes) of thyme and $\frac{1}{2}$ oz (14 grammes) of mint. Add 1 oz (28 grammes) of dried salt and $\frac{1}{4}$ oz (7 grammes) of ground cloves and another $\frac{1}{4}$ oz (7 grammes) of caraway seeds. Mix all well together with your hands.

Make bags about 4 inches (10 cm) square of fairly loosely woven cotton material. Fill them with the lavender mixture and finish off the last side securely. The bags can be placed in drawers as they are or hung from coat hangers with a loop of ribbon.

Perfumed sachets

Another kind of fragrant sachet can be made for your drawers and wardrobes with 1 oz (28 grammes) each of cloves, caraway seeds, nutmeg, mace, cinnamon and tonquin beans ground up and mixed with 6 oz (168 grammes) of Florentine orris root. Sachets filled with this mixture are reputed to keep moths away.

PATCHWORK

Once you become skilful at patchwork you can use it to make all kinds of things – evening skirts, dresses, hats, shopping bags, tea-cosies are only a few – but perhaps cushion covers, bedcovers or wall hangings are the easiest shapes to start with. If you want to work in large patchwork pieces with heavy material it is better to make a bedcover rather than a cushion cover, but if you are using cotton or silk pieces, your patchwork would be best made into smaller articles.

The pieces are cut out round templates, usually hexagonal, though squares and other shapes can also be used. Make your first template on a piece of heavy card that will stand up to a great deal of wear. To make a hexagon, draw with a pair of compasses a circle roughly the size you want your patches to be. Keeping your compasses as they are, place the point on the circumference of the circle and make a pencil mark where the arc cuts the circumference. Place the point

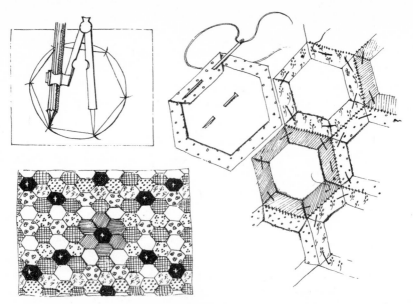

on that mark and cut the circumference again. Continue until you are back where you started. Join up the pencil marks and you will have a hexagon.

This hexagon is your main template. Before you begin work cut out quite a number of identical shapes in thin card (old Christmas cards are ideal for this). Take your thin templates and, one at a time, cut out patches from the material making sure that you allow at least $\frac{1}{2}$ inch (1 cm) extra all round for turning in. Tack each patch onto a thin card template making a neat and close turn over of the material.

When you have made about a dozen, take two, lay them together with the right sides facing and, using overstitch, sew them together along one side of the hexagon. Take a third patch, place it so that it touches the first two on two sides. Stitch it first to one, then to the other. Always work in overstitch and always remember to work on the wrong side. Continue adding patches and give a lot of attention to the mixing of your colours. For the time being leave your templates in the material. When you run out of patches, make another dozen or so, using your first strong template to cut the thinner card again.

When the patchwork is as large as you want it to be, search all over it carefully for any weaknesses in the stitching and make certain that all fastening off has been well done. Remove the tacking threads and take out the templates. Press the patchwork lightly on the right side with a damp cloth. Line it with a suitable plain fabric, turning in the patchwork over the lining about 1 inch (2·5 cm).

SCENTED PILLOWS

Rose Pillows

Collect your rose petals after the dew has gone on a dry day. Put them on white paper to dry in the sunshine and keep turning them over to make sure that all the moisture dries out. Make a bag of muslin or fine cotton and pour the petals into it. Sprinkle them with powdered orris root, mixing it well in with your hands and crumble the brittle rose petals finely. Keep adding rose petals and orris root until the pillow is nice and plump; then sew it up with close, small stitches. Make a cover for your rose pillow and you'll find its fragrance gives you a great deal of pleasure.

Lavender Pillows

Collect and dry lavender flowers in the same way as for rose pillows, but this time add 1 oz (28 grammes) each of ground cinnamon and cloves, 2 oz (56 grammes) of powdered orris root and $\frac{1}{2}$ oz (14 grammes) of musk to every 1 lb of dried lavender flowers. Store the mixture in jars with screw-top lids for a fortnight to allow it to mature. Then, as with the rose pillow, make an inner case of fine cotton, sew it up with small, close stitches and make an attractive cover for it.

Herb Pillows

Herb pillows are often recommended as a cure for insomnia, but whether or not they have this effect, they are a source of pleasure to people who do not sleep well for they retain their fragrance for months.

Take four layers of cotton wool each the size of a pillow. Make them soft and fluffy. Lay out three on a table and sprinkle them liberally with handfuls of dried herbs and dried scented leaves. Choose those that have a strong perfume like mint and thyme, rosemary, bay, mint and southernwood. Then pile the three layers one on top of the other, and place the fourth one on top so that the herbs are all enclosed within the cotton wool. Stitch with large stitches all round the edge of the pillow and run a few stitches across it to keep the layers in place. Make a fine cotton inner cover as well as the pillow-case.

RAG RUG

Rag rugs, made of strips cut from old clothes, have long been used in English villages. These rugs stand up to wear, and frequent shakings and mild beatings keep them looking well. They are made by pushing individual strips about 1 inch by $3\frac{3}{4}$ inches (2.5 cm by 9.5 cm) through sacking. The tool used for these rugs can still be

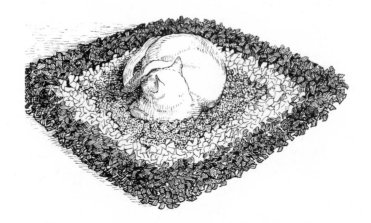

bought, but you can make a perfectly adequate one by removing one prong from a wooden clothes peg and shaping the one that remains so that it can easily penetrate the sacking. Use a pen-knife to shape it and then rub it down with sandpaper.

Many of the rugs still to be seen in cottages are made of strips of dark coloured cloth from coats and jackets. This is because the woollen material from which such garments are made stays firmly in the sacking and is also hard-wearing. But strong cotton material can also be used and you are more likely to find this in bright colours.

When you choose garments for cutting up, make certain they are of similar texture and that you will get enough strips to carry out a design. Circles of bright colour look very attractive in the centre of rectangular rugs for example. However, if you do not have sufficient strips to carry out a pattern, use colours at random and your rug will still look most attractive. Plenty that still lie before country hearths were made like this.

Wash the sacking, open the seams and cut a shape just 1 inch (2.5 cm) bigger all round than you want your rug to be. Turn in the hem and tack it down with large stitches. If you want to work a design, draw this on the sacking with chalk or a felt-tipped pen. Working from the back, push one end of a strip through to the right side of the rug. A $\frac{1}{2}$ inch (1·25 cm) further on, push the other end through to the right side as well, then push one end of a new strip through the

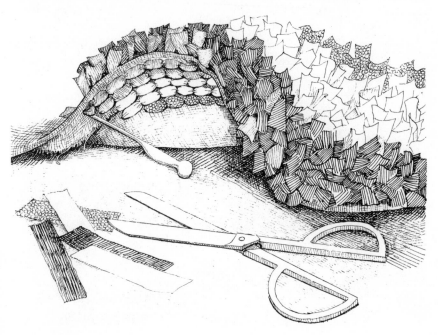

same hole. The other end of the second strip goes through $\frac{1}{2}$ inch (1·25 cm) further on. Continue like this using different colours to work out your design, or else introducing your colours at random.

When the sacking is completely covered, trim the pile with sharp scissors so that it is even. Use another piece of sacking to back the rug, turning in the edges and hemming them neatly with strong thread. The backing gives the rug extra weight and strength.

CROCHETED RAG RUGS

Crocheted rag rugs are best made with long strips of lightweight cotton material in contrasting colours. You may have garments you can cut up or you may find suitable remnants in the shops. You need a lot of material and it's worth bearing in mind that the longer your strips, the fewer joins there are to make.

The crochet hook is size 7 and you'll need a pair of sharp scissors unless you are able to tear your material into strips. The strips have to be about $1\frac{1}{2}$ inches (3.5 cm) wide and as long as possible. Pay a great deal of attention to the colours of the material you choose as these rugs are normally worked either in stripes or in concentric circles and the most striking effects are achieved with contrasting plain colours.

A striped rug

This is the easier rug to make. Make a chain about the width you intend for your rug, then continue in double crochet until your first band of colour is complete. Whenever you have to make joins, tie the two ends together at the beginning of a row. Cut the ends short and tuck them neatly into the back of the rug.

Similarly, always introduce a new colour at the beginning of a row and tuck the two ends into the back of the rug.

Continue in double crochet varying the widths of the bands of colour until the rug is as long as you want it to be. Fasten off at the end of a row with a slip stitch and tuck the end into the back as before. Make certain it cannot come undone.

Lay out the rug on a flat surface and cover it with a damp sheet. Leave it to dry. The rug will then be flat and smooth.

A circular rug

Begin the circular rug by working 6 chain stitches into the 1st chain to form a ring.

1st round Work 2 double crochets into each chain to make 12 stitches. End with a slip-stitch into the 1st double crochet.

2nd round *1 double crochet into the 1st stitch, 2 double crochets

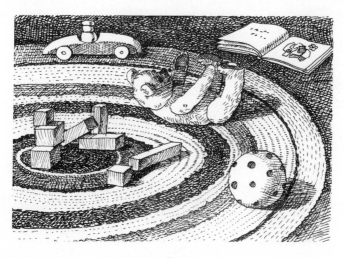

into the next stitch *. Repeat from * to * and end with a slip stitch into the 1st double crochet.

3rd round *1 double crochet into the next 2 double crochets, 2 double crochets into the next double crochet *. Repeat from * to * ending with a slip stitch into the 1st double crochet.

Continue crocheting in a circle, increasing to bring the rug to the size you want, but be careful to keep it flat. Whenever you want to make a join in order to continue a colour or to change to another one, tie the ends together firmly and tuck them as neatly as possible into the back of the rug. Fasten off with a slip stitch when the rug is complete and tuck the end in.

Lay the rug on a flat surface under a damp sheet to smooth it out.

SAMPLERS

Centuries ago samplers were worked as reference panels of embroidery stitches. Those that have survived from the first part of the seventeenth century are nearly always in coloured silks and metal thread on long, loosely-woven pieces of linen. Later in that century they seem to have become shorter, and the stitching is used to create birds, flowers, animals and geometrical designs. The linen is finer and the silks paler in colour. By the eighteenth century the sampler has become a child's exercise, and is squarer in shape. It sets the imagination wandering to see the young needlewoman's age and name worked in careful stitches. Alphabets are there too and texts, as well as trees, flowers, and simple designs. One hopes to find a date on such a sampler, but, sad to say, it is not always there. The most common stitch used is cross stitch.

Choose a loosely woven piece of material with a regular and even warp and weft for your own sampler. Work out a design and the placing of your wording in detail on squared paper. Do this with coloured pencils; you will then see exactly what effect you are going to achieve.

If you tack your material on to an old picture frame you will find that you can work more easily. Whenever you change your thread, try to finish off very neatly at the back. Even with a simple cross

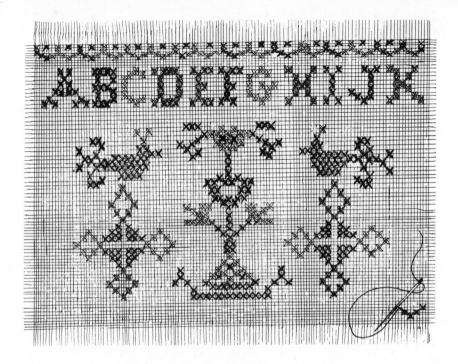

stitch you will find you can embroider houses, trees, flowers and all kinds of other things, so it is worth trying to create a personal record just as the earlier sampler-makers did. But don't forget to embroider the date.

SMOCKING

Smocking describes the particular kind of embroidery used on garments known as smocks. These were worn by women in the Anglo-Saxon period. Saxon women wore them as undergarments together with breeches and a dress, but later, when the gathered fullness of smocks began to be decorated with embroidery, the dresses were cut low to show it off. Later on still, the strong linen smock-frock, a kind of overall, became the accepted wear of English country labourers and tradesmen. Women went on using smocking on their dresses and blouses to decorate gathered material at the neck, yoke and sleeves.

Linen was the fabric commonly used to make smock-frocks. White linen was favoured in the Home Counties, dark blue in the Midlands. Drab green was preferred in Hertfordshire and in Essex and Cambridge too. In the Isle of Wight, black linen with white embroidery was popular, and in Dorset, the linen was grey and the embroidery was blue and white. But Sunday wear, over the whole

country, was, it seems, white linen with white embroidery. The motif worked into the embroidery sometimes showed the wearer's trade, so a woodman would have trees on his smock-frock, while a carter would have cartwheels.

Many of the materials chosen by women for their smocked garments would be difficult to find today. Spun silk, holland, tussore, chiffon, crêpe-de-chine, muslin and ninon have given way to nylon, viyella, perlon and polyester-cotton, but these new fabrics have the quality that is essential for smocking – they gather well – so there is no reason why they should not be used with the same success.

Since it is important that the fullness of the material of any garment you want to decorate with smocking is gathered evenly, it's worth buying a smocking transfer from a needlecraft shop. The transfer will give you rows of perfectly spaced dots which will guide you in your gathering.

Of course, the smocking has to be done before the garment is made up. Pin the transfer on to the wrong side of the material and iron an extra row of dots at the top, and one more dot along each line than the stitches you intend to work require. (The top row is gathered along with the rest so that the neck or yoke can be sewn on to it; the extra dot on each line is necessary because you work the gathering on the wrong side and need to make an extra pleat.)

Fasten your thread both with a knot and a double stitch on the right-hand end of the first row of dots and remember that you should be working on the wrong side of the material. To ensure even gathering insert your needle immediately on the right-hand side of the first dot and bring it out immediately on the left-hand side of the same dot. Repeat this all the way along the line. Leave a long thread at the end. Start the next line of gathers again at the right-hand side with new thread, inserting the needle immediately on the right-hand side of the first dot in the second row. Gather as before. At the end of the line, loosely tie the two free ends of thread together. Repeat this along every line of dots, tying each pair of threads together in such a way that they cannot slip, but can be undone later.

Now gather up the material into pleats, but not too tightly as this would prevent the work from 'giving' and anyway the pleats must be movable so that the needle can go between them when the smocking is being worked. Keep the threads tied and the pleats in position with a few pins at the end of the rows. The preparation for smocking is now complete.

The embroidery is worked in stranded cotton. Give careful attention to the colours chosen and to how they will look on the material of the garment. There are many traditional stitches. Only a few simple ones are given here.

Outline Stitch

Many patterns begin with this stitch. Bring your needle left of the 1st pleat at the top left-hand side of the gathering. (You are now working on the right side of the garment and you embroider from left to right.)

Slant the needle as shown in the diagram and pick up the next pleat to the right. Keep the thread above the needle. Repeat this with each pleat in turn. Fasten off neatly at the end of the row on the wrong side of the work.

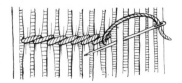

Further rows of outline stitch can be worked under the first one or a different stitch can be used.

Cable Stitch

This stitch is as simple as outline stitch, but you insert the needle horizontally and hold the thread alternately above and below the needle.

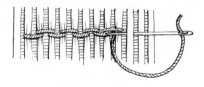

Double Cable Stitch

A second row of cable stitch worked close to the first one gives you double cable stitch.

Diamond Stitch

Work begins halfway between two gathering threads for diamond stitch. Bring up your needle at the

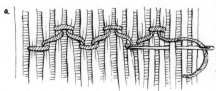

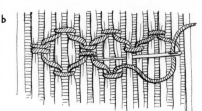

first pleat on the left-hand side and take one stitch on this with the thread held above the needle, followed by one in the 2nd pleat beside the first stitch with the thread held below the needle. Take your needle upwards to the 1st gathering thread and take one stitch in the 3rd pleat with the thread below the needle, followed by another in the 4th pleat beside the 3rd pleat with the thread above the needle. Take your needle down again level with the 1st stitch and take a stitch in the 5th pleat with the thread above the needle, followed by a stitch beside it in the 6th pleat with the thread below the needle. Continue in this way pleat by pleat all along the row (diagram a).

The other half of the diamond is formed by starting immediately below the 1st stitch and placing subsequent stitches correctly in relation to the first half of the diamond, as shown in diagram b.

Honeycomb Stitch

Bring your needle up in the 1st pleat then take a stitch through the top of the 2nd and 1st pleats together. Catch them firmly together

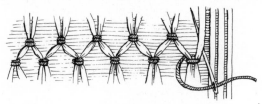

with a second stitch, but this time carry the needle on down the back of the 2nd pleat until the 2nd gathering thread is reached. Catch the 3rd and 2nd pleats together with a stitch. Catch them again before taking the needle up the back of the 3rd pleat and out at the first gathering thread. Continue working up and down like this all the way along the row. Work subsequent rows of honeycomb stitch on two gathering threads in the same way.

Build up a pattern of stitches until you have worked as much smocking as you require. Give your work a good finish by laying it face downwards with a damp cloth over it and passing an iron gently over it until the dampness has gone. Never press down with the iron.

4 · Home-made cosmetics

Bath crystals · Bath salts · Herb bath · Scented bath · Mustard bath · Treatment for dry hair · Hair care · Hair wash · Hair colourant · Hand softener · Hand lotion · Hand care · Treatment for hands and nails · Eye lotion · Eyelash care · Cold cream · Face cream · Cleansing cream · Anti-freckles cream · Face pack – 1 and 2 · Astringent lotion – 1 and 2 · Cleansing lotion · Treatment for a greasy skin · Face conditioner · Sun-tan lotion · Sunburn lotion

BATH CRYSTALS

To make these you need 1 lb (½ kilo) of carbonate of soda crystals, one teaspoonful of oil of lavender and, if possible, one teaspoonful of another flower or herb oil, and a large glass jar with a closely fitting glass lid.

Put a layer of soda crystals at the bottom of the jar and add a few drops of oil. Close the lid and shake the jar gently. The next day add more crystals and a few more drops of oil. Continue like this until all the crystals and oil are used.

Shake the jar gently, seal it and leave the crystals at least three months before using them.

BATH SALTS

Dilute blue vegetable dye and mix it gradually in a large bowl with 7 lb (3½ kilos) of sesquicarbonate. When you have distributed the colour evenly and have achieved an attractive shade of pale blue or mauve stir in lavender oil so that it too is evenly distributed. There are other oils available (rose-geranium, rosemary and sandalwood) that might well be used with different coloured vegetable dyes.

HERB BATH

Make a 6 inch (15 cm) square muslin bag, hem it at the opening and insert a draw string. Put in 2 oz (56 grammes) of lavender flowers, 1 oz (28 grammes) of lemon thyme, 1 oz (28 grammes) of common thyme, 1 oz (28 grammes) of crushed poppy heads and enough brewer's hops to fill up the bag to within 2 inches (5 cm) of the top.

Draw up the string and wind it securely round the top of the bag (do not tie it, as you will want to add more herbs from time to time). Hang the bag from the tap so that it is entirely immersed in the bath water. Squeeze the bag well and set it aside. After bathing hang it to dry in the open air. After several baths, throw away the herbs and fill the bag with fresh ones.

SCENTED BATH

Make a muslin bag with a draw-string neck and put in 1 oz (28 grammes) of dried rose, verbena or freesia petals, 1 oz (28 grammes) of lavender flowers or orris root and the grated rind of a

lemon. Hang the bag from the tap to allow it to scent the bathwater and squeeze it before removing it. After bathing, hang the bag to dry in the open air so that its contents do not become musty. Refill the bag after it has been used several times.

MUSTARD BATH

A mustard bath is comforting and is thought a good thing to take if you have a chill coming on. In a bowl mix 2 oz (56 grammes) of mustard for every 3 gallons (14 litres) of water your bath will contain. Pour this into a really hot bath.

TREATMENT FOR DRY HAIR

If in spite of regular brushing your hair is dry and brittle, part the hair and apply a few drops of olive oil or almond oil directly on to the scalp with a small piece of sponge. Rub it well into the roots of the hair. Continue with this treatment for about ten days.

HAIR CARE

Nourish your hair by rubbing in olive oil. Wrap your head in a hot towel and leave the oil on for several hours. This treatment every few weeks will keep your hair in good condition.

Honey can be added to olive oil in the proportion of one part to two as another way of nourishing hair. Warm the mixture in a bowl which is standing in a pan of hot water. Stir it well and massage it into the head. Wrap your head in a hot towel for 20 minutes.

Shampoo the hair afterwards.

HAIR WASH

Reduce 1 oz (28 grammes) of borax and ½ oz (14 grammes) of camphor to a fine powder. Dissolve them in 1 quart (1 litre) of boiling water. Allow the solution to cool and use it instead of shampoo. This mixture is said not only to cleanse, strengthen and beautify hair, but also to preserve its colour and prevent early baldness!

HAIR COLOURANT

Put 1 tablespoonful of tea and 1 tablespoonful of dried sage into a basin, cover them with boiling water and simmer the basin in a saucepan with a lid for two hours. Cool the lotion and strain it.

Rub this lotion into your scalp four or five times a week and greyness will gradually disappear. The hair goes dark brown.

Make a fresh supply of the lotion each week.

HAND SOFTENER

Shake up equal portions of spirits of ammonia and glycerine in a screw-topped jar. Moisten your hands with this mixture each night and you will find that not only does it soften and whiten them, but it also stops them from chapping.

HAND LOTION

Equal quantities of extract of witch-hazel, glycerine and eau-de-cologne shaken well together make a good hand lotion for regular use.

HAND CARE

Lemon juice rubbed on the hands keeps them soft and prevents them from chapping.

TREATMENT FOR HANDS AND NAILS

Immerse the fingers in a cup of warm olive oil to which lemon juice has been added. This is a good treatment for nails that break and for keeping your hands soft.

EYE LOTION

Put a good handful of cornflowers into a basin and pour 1 pint ($\frac{1}{2}$ litre) of boiling water on them. Leave to brew for a few minutes. Strain the lotion and leave it to cool. Dip cotton wool into the lotion and bathe the eyes.

EYELASH CARE

Pure olive oil or melted vaseline will make eyelashes grow. Remove any powder or mascara from your eyelashes and apply the oil or vaseline with a fine camel-hair brush. Do this regularly, brushing the top lashes upwards and the lower ones downwards.

COLD CREAM

Put 4 oz (113 grammes) of almond oil and 1 oz (28 grammes) of pure lanolin into a basin standing in a saucepan of boiling water. Stir the mixture vigorously with a bone or porcelain spoon. When it is almost cool, beat in $\frac{1}{2}$ drachm (1 gramme) of borax and 2 oz (56 grammes) of rosewater.

Store in jars or pots with screw-top lids.

FACE CREAM

Beat the white of an egg until it is firm and add one dessertspoonful of honey and a few drops of almond oil. Continue beating until the ingredients combine to make a fine, smooth cream.

For this cream you will need 4 oz (113 grammes) of almond oil, 1½ oz (42 grammes) of white bees-wax, 2 oz (56 grammes) of diluted rosewater, a small pinch of purified borax, half a teaspoonful of glycerine and a few drops of oil of roses.

Shred the beeswax finely and put it in a stone jar. Put the almond oil in another jar and the rosewater, borax and glycerine in a third. Stand all three in a large pan which is heating slowly. When the wax melts stir it into the oil with a bone spoon. Add the contents of the third jar slowly stirring all the time. Remove from the heat and leave the cream to cool. As it begins to thicken, add the oil of roses.

ANTI-FRECKLE CREAM

Mix well together 1 oz (28 grammes) of fresh lemon juice, ¼ teaspoonful of powdered borax and ½ drachm (1 gramme) of oil of rosemary. Put the cream in a jar with a screw top and leave it to stand for a few days. Use it on the hands and face and it will lighten freckles and then cause them to disappear.

FACE PACK – I

Cleanse the skin with warm water and pat it dry with a soft cloth. Make a thick creamy paste by heating about a gill and a half (20 centilitres) of milk in a double saucepan and stirring in one teaspoonful of ground almonds and enough fuller's earth to thicken it. Leave it until it is just warm and then spread it all over the face and neck, avoiding the eyes and eyelids. Lie down and rest until the paste dries and begins to flake off when the face muscles are moved.

The face pack comes away with a soft cloth dipped in warm water.

This treatment can be followed every two weeks to cleanse your face and tone up the skin.

Beat the white of an egg until it is firm and mix in a small amount of fine oatmeal. Spread this paste over the face and neck, avoiding the eyes and eyelashes. Leave it to dry. Rinse it off with lukewarm water and tone up the skin afterwards with an astringent lotion.

ASTRINGENT LOTION – I

Use witch-hazel diluted with an equal quantity of water to make an astringent lotion for closing the pores of the face. This is a good lotion to use after cleansing your skin by steaming it over a basin of hot water.

ASTRINGENT LOTION – 2

All herbs with astringent properties such as thyme, rosemary, bramble and hawthorn leaves can be infused to make skin lotions.

CLEANSING LOTION

Add a few drops of eau-de-cologne to fresh milk to make a beneficial and inexpensive cleansing lotion.

TREATMENT FOR A GREASY SKIN

Apply the white of an egg to your face if you have trouble with a greasy skin.

FACE CONDITIONER

A couple of hours before going to bed mix flowers of sulphur and milk in a wine glass. Without disturbing the sulphur, apply the milk to your skin and leave it on overnight. This mixture does not keep so make it fresh each evening.

SUN-TAN LOTION

Shake together vigorously ½ pint (¼ litre) of pure olive oil, 10 drops of tincture of iodine and the juice of a lemon. This lotion, when applied to the skin before sun-bathing, will help to give you a good tan, while keeping your skin supple.

SUNBURN LOTION

Take equal parts of rose water and glycerine and add an equivalent quantity of juice squeezed from a fresh cucumber. Dab this lotion gently on to the sunburned area of the skin.

5 · Cleaning tips

*Boards · Bottles · Brass · Cane chairs and tables · Clocks · Fish
saucepans and utensils · Furniture · Furs · Glass and china ·
Grease stains on the hearth · Hairbrushes · Ivory · Jewellery ·
Keys and locks · Leather · Marble · Marcasite jewellery · Mirrors
and windows · Papier-mâché · Piano keys · Picture frames ·
Playing cards · Rugs · Sewing machines · Soft furniture · Spectacles · Straw matting · Suede · Tar stains · Tennis balls · Velvet ·
Wallpaper · Wine glasses and tumblers · Wine stains · Wrought
iron*

BOARDS

Mix three parts of fine sand with one part of lime. Apply this with a scrubbing-brush. This mixture removes grease and whitens boards. Rinse off with clean water.

BOTTLES

Crush the shell of an egg and drop it in the bottle. Add a little hot water and swill it round. This will get rid of discolouration.

BRASS

A mixture of salt and vinegar applied on a soft cloth cleans brass well.

CANE CHAIRS AND TABLES

These should be washed with hot soap suds and dried in the open air.

CLOCKS

Soak a piece of cotton-wool in paraffin oil and place it on a small receptacle inside the clock case underneath the works. Close the case and, if the clock is dusty, the fumes of the paraffin will bring down the particles of dust on to the cotton-wool. Leave the clock closed up for 24 hours, then remove the cotton-wool.

FISH SAUCEPANS AND UTENSILS

After washing these, any fishy smell that remains will soon disappear if you sprinkle dry mustard on them and rub it in with a wet rag. Rinse off with warm water.

FURNITURE

When wooden furniture needs cleaning wring out a cloth that has been dampened in a mixture of warm water and a little vinegar and rub vigorously with it.

Oak furniture can be cleaned with warm beer.

Moisten bran with hot water and rub it well into the fur. Dry by rubbing first with towelling and then with fine muslin and some dry bran. Take the fur into the open and shake well, then hang it on the line.

GLASS AND CHINA

Dissolve borax in hot water and leave it to cool. This solution is useful for cleaning all glass and china and it leaves them particularly shiny.

GREASE STAINS ON THE HEARTH

These should be covered immediately with thick, hot ashes.

HAIRBRUSHES

Add borax to hot water in a wash basin and swish the brush about vigorously. Keep the back of the brush and the handle dry. Place the brush, bristle downwards, on a dry towel.

IVORY

A paste made of sal volatile and olive oil cleans ivory very well. Rub the mixture on to the ivory and leave it in the sun to dry. Brush it off carefully and polish with a soft duster.

JEWELLERY

Wash jewellery in a plastic bowl in pure soap suds. Dry it with a soft cloth and finish with soft leather.

KEYS AND LOCKS

Rusty keys and locks can be placed in paraffin oil. The oil loosens the rust and it then rubs off quite easily.

LEATHER

Dampen a cloth and rub the leather and then dry it with another cloth. Beat the white of an egg to a stiff froth and spread it over the leather. Wipe this off and the leather will look much fresher.

MARBLE

Take two parts of soda to one of pumice-stone and one of finely powdered chalk. Sift these through a fine sieve and mix them to a paste with water. This will clean marble. Wash it off with soap and water.

Another method is to make a paste of chloride of lime and water and rub it into the stains with an old cloth. Continue the applications until the stains disappear. Wash off with soapy water and buff with a soft cloth.

MARCASITE JEWELLERY

Marcasite jewellery should never be cleaned with water.

Dip a fine brush in silver cleaning liquid and leave it to dry. Place the piece of marcasite on a piece of soft cloth and work it over with the dry brush until it shines.

MIRRORS AND WINDOWS

Methylated spirit on a clean cloth will clean mirrors and windows and leaves no smears. Newspaper dipped in a water and vinegar solution will also clean windows and mirrors.

PAPIER-MÂCHÉ

Anything made of papier-mâché should be sponged with cold water and sprinkled with flour while it is damp. Leave it a few minutes then wipe off the flour and polish with a clean, dry duster.

PIANO KEYS

Make a paste of powdered whiting and methylated spirit. Apply to the keys with a soft cloth. Polish it off with silky textured material.

PICTURE FRAMES

Gilt frames can be cleaned with a rag dampened in very weak ammonia water. Buff them afterwards with a soft, dry cloth.

PLAYING CARDS

Lay the cards out on a piece of cloth and sprinkle them with talcum powder on both sides. Then rub them lightly with a soft, dry cloth.

RUGS

A rug is freshened by dragging it across grass with the pile downwards. Shake it well and hang it over a line for a while.

SEWING MACHINES

If your sewing machine gets clogged up pour paraffin oil over the working parts and then wipe it away with a rag. Use a soft pipe-cleaner dipped in paraffin to get to inaccessible parts.

SOFT FURNITURE

Rub this with a warm, dampened flannel dipped in bran.

SPECTACLES

Make a lotion from one tablespoonful of glycerine and half a cup of methylated spirit. Put it into a bottle and shake it up well. A few drops on a soft cloth will clean your spectacles. Store the lotion, but keep a cap or top on the bottle.

STRAW MATTING

Wipe this with a large, coarse cloth using water to which salt has been added. The salt stops the matting from turning yellow.

SUEDE

This can be freshened by dipping a slightly damp flannel in bran and rubbing it into the garment. Then shake well and rub lightly with fine sandpaper to restore the pile.

TAR STAINS

Make a paste of turpentine and powdered fuller's earth. Rub this over the tar and leave it to dry. Brush off the powdery residue when it is absolutely dry.

TENNIS BALLS

These can be scrubbed in hot soapy water and, after rinsing, left in the sun to dry.

VELVET

Grease stains can be taken out of velvet by soaking the spot with turpentine. Rub it dry with a clean flannel. Repeat this process if the spot still shows. Then brush it well and hang the garment out in the air to get rid of the smell of the turpentine.

WALLPAPER

Cut a very stale white loaf of bread into slices and wipe them lightly over the wallpaper. Use downward strokes and clean about a square yard at a time. Be careful to leave no marks.

WINE GLASSES AND TUMBLERS

Add a little ammonia to the washing water and rinse in clean, cold water. Polish with a soft tea-towel.

WINE STAINS

If a wine stain is immersed in boiling milk it will soon disappear.

WROUGHT IRON

Rub with a cloth dipped in a light oil and polish with a dry cloth.

6 · Helpful hints

Sewing on buttons · To make candles last longer · Treating sagging cane chair seats · Treating a worn carpet · Cramp · Removing creases from clothes · Making flowers last · Furniture cream · Furniture polish · To loosen glass stoppers · To remove grass stains from white material · Heat marks on the table · To remove iron-rust stains · To freshen a lettuce · Cleaning a mincing machine · Mosquito bites · Mustard · Onion smells · Paint stains Hanging pictures · To soften boot and furniture polish · Rice water · Burned saucepans · Treatment for scratches · Damp shoes · Making a silver cloth · Silver cleaning by immersion · Softening water · Sponges · To stiffen a straw hat · Wallpaper patches · Wasp stings · Restoring velvet · To remove wax from a table-cloth

SEWING ON BUTTONS

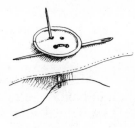

Place a darning needle under buttons before you sew them on. The button will not be so tightly fixed to the material and stays on better.

TO MAKE CANDLES LAST LONGER

Coat candles with a light varnish and leave them to dry. The varnish forms a hard edging which holds the molten grease longer.

TREATING SAGGING CANE CHAIR SEATS

Wash a sagging cane chair seat in hot water and soda, but be careful to avoid touching the wood of the chair with the hot water. Wipe it and stand the chair to dry in a current of air.

TREATING A WORN CARPET

Small threadbare patches can be disguised effectively by simulating the pattern with coloured inks.

CRAMP

Thread a cork on to a loose anklet and wear it in bed if you are subject to cramp.

REMOVING CREASES FROM CLOTHES

Hang clothes that are creased over a bath of steaming hot water.

MAKING FLOWERS LAST

In hot weather place cut flowers in vases made of pottery rather than glass, since the water will stay cooler. Remember to snip off a little piece from the end of each stalk when changing the water. When the flowers begin to droop an aspirin will revive them.

FURNITURE CREAM

Mix together in a screw-topped jar ½ pint (300 ml) of linseed oil and 1½ cups of methylated spirit. Always shake this cream before using it. Apply with a soft pad and buff with a soft duster.

FURNITURE POLISH

Bring 1 oz (28 grammes) of white soap to the boil in half a pint of water. Leave this to cool. Stand 1 oz (28 grammes) of shredded white wax and 1 oz (28 grammes) of shredded bees-wax in half a pint (300 ml) of turpentine overnight. In the morning mix the two liquids together and beat them until you have a creamy white polish.

TO LOOSEN GLASS STOPPERS

Pour a little salad oil round the stopper and put the bottle where the heat from a fire can just reach it. Tap gently round the stopper with a wooden instrument wrapped in a duster. The heat will cause the oil to work round the stopper and it should come out easily after a while.

Smear a little glycerine on the stopper before replacing it to stop it sticking again.

TO REMOVE GRASS STAINS FROM WHITE MATERIAL

Rub the stain with methylated spirits and then wash the garment in the usual way.

HEAT MARKS ON TABLES

Make a thin paste of salad oil and salt, rub it well into the affected area of wood and leave it to stand for an hour or so. Polish the surface afterwards with a soft cloth.

TO REMOVE IRON-RUST STAINS

Moisten salt with lemon juice and apply it to the iron-rust stain. Leave it there for some time. Repeat the applications until the stain disappears. Rinse several times in cold water and then give a final rinse in water to which a little ammonia has been added.

TO FRESHEN A LETTUCE

Always keep a small piece of washed coal in a jam jar in your kitchen. Before using the lettuce soak it in a bowl of cold water in which the coal is immersed.

CLEANING A MINCING MACHINE

Grind some pieces of stale bread through the machine before taking it to pieces. This will collect grease, fat and skin. Wipe all the parts with a clean cloth after this.

MOSQUITO BITES

Apply moist toilet soap to the bite.

MUSTARD

Mustard made with vinegar will last longer than that made with water.

ONION SMELLS

Rub in raw celery or parsley to remove smell of onions from the hands.

PAINT STAINS

Equal parts of ammonia and turpentine will remove paint from clothes. First soak the area in the solution, then wash the garment in the usual way.

HANGING PICTURES

A sliver of cork glued at each side of the bottom of a picture frame keeps the picture off the wall and prevents a dark line forming on the wallpaper or emulsion paint. This also stops damp affecting the picture.

TO SOFTEN BOOT AND FURNITURE POLISH

If the lid has been left off the tin and the polish has hardened, soften it by adding a few drops of turpentine and stirring it round with a stick.

RICE WATER

The water in which rice has been cooked can be used for thickening soup; it can also serve as a substitute for light starch.

BURNED SAUCEPANS

If you burn a saucepan, clean off as much as you can, then put in a handful of salt and fill with cold water. Leave it to stand for an hour or so.

TREATMENT FOR SCRATCHES

Surface scratches on furniture should be treated with a mixture of equal parts of linseed oil and turpentine. Rub this well into the scratches and then polish with a soft duster.

The best way of treating furniture made from walnut is to crush a piece of walnut and rub it into the scratch.

DAMP SHOES

A few drops of paraffin added to the polish helps to give a shine to damp shoes.

MAKING A SILVER CLOTH

Mix well together 1 tablespoonful of plate powder, 1 tablespoonful of cloudy ammonia and 1 pint (½ litre) of water. Take a loosely woven tea towel or a piece of turkish towelling and soak it in the mixture. Hang up the towel to dry, but do not wring it at all.

When the cloth is dry store it in a plastic bag and use it for drying silver that has been washed in the usual way. A silver cloth prepared in this way will last for several months. Another solution recommended for this method consists of 1 tablespoonful of plate powder, 2 tablespoonsful of methylated spirit and ½ pint (¼ litre) of boiling water.

SILVER CLEANING BY IMMERSION

Dissolve a teaspoonful of salt and a teaspoonful of soda in boiling water. Add small pieces of aluminium (keep some handy for this purpose). Immerse the silver in the solution and make sure that it touches the aluminium. Remove the silver and rub it dry.

SOFTENING WATER

Add a tablespoonful of borax to each gallon of washing water to soften it. You will then need to use less washing powder.

SPONGES

A soaking for a few hours in vinegar will thoroughly clean sponges that have become slimy. Rinse several times in hot water afterwards.

TO STIFFEN A STRAW HAT

Brush it well to remove any dust. Put 4 tablespoonsful of boiling water into a bowl and add 4 lumps of sugar. Apply this solution to the hat with a stiff brush.

WALLPAPER PATCHES

If you need to put a patch on your wallpaper do not cut a neat shape but tear a ragged piece, if possible with the under edges thinner. This kind of patch shows less.

WASP STINGS

Apply diluted vinegar to the sting.

RESTORING VELVET

Velvet which has been crushed should be held over a basin of hot water with the pile facing the rising steam.

TO REMOVE WAX FROM A TABLE-CLOTH

Scrape off as much of the wax as you can. Place a piece of white blotting-paper over the mark and hold a hot iron an inch or two above it. The blotting paper will absorb the wax as it melts.

Further reading

Practical Rushwork by Norah Florance (Dryad Press)
Rush Baskets and Mats, Illustrated Leaflet No. 112 (Dryad Press)
The Junior Basket Maker by Charles Crampton (Dryad Press)
Canework by Charles Crampton (Dryad Press)
Willow Basket Work by A. G. Knock (Dryad Press)
The Craft of Straw Decoration by Alec Coker (Dryad Press)
The New Golden Dolly by Minnie Lambeth (John Baker)
English Smocks by Alice Armes (Dryad Press)
Beginning Patchwork by Dorothy Wright (Dryad Press)
Your Book of Patchwork by Priscilla Lobley (Faber & Faber)
Basic Crochet (Leaflet) by Dorothy Standing (N.F.W.I. Publication*)
Uses and Pleasures of Herbs by Sheila M. Chase (Bedford Federation of
    W.I.'s, W.I. House, 62 Adelaide Square, Bedford MK40 2RW)
Preserving Flowers and Foliage (N.F.W.I. Publication*)
Guide to Craft Supplies by Judy Allen (Studio Vista, 1974)

*N.F.W.I. Sales Department, 39 Eccleston Street, London SW1W
9NT.

The Council for Small Industries in Rural Areas has an Advisory
Services Division at 35 Camp Road, Wimbledon Common,
London SW19 4UP. The CoSIRA guide to Country Workshops
in Britain lists over a thousand country craft workshops and retail
shops. This is available from bookshops.

Suppliers of herbs and handicraft materials

HERBAL SUPPLIERS

Culpeper Ltd.
21 Bruton Street
London W1X 7DH

Madge Hooper, F.R.H.S.
Stoke-Lacy Herb Farm
Bromyard
Herefordshire

The Herb Shop
The American Museum
Claverton Manor
Bath, Somerset

HANDICRAFT MATERIALS

Dryad
Northgates
Leicester LE1 4QR

Smith & Co. Ltd.
99 Walnut Tree Close
Guildford
Surrey GU1 4UQ

Nottingham Handicraft Co.
Melton Road
West Bridgford
Nottingham

Gray and Carhill
112 Queens Road
Peckham
London SE15 2QU

Jacobs, Young & Westbury Ltd.*
J.Y.W. House
Bridge Road
Haywards Heath
Sussex RH16 1TZ
* Suppliers of rushes

List of museums

The Castle Museum, York
The American Museum, Claverton Manor, Bath, Somerset
Tudor House Museum, Southampton
Northampton Museum, Northampton
Red House Museum and Art Gallery, Christchurch, Hants
The London Museum at Kensington Palace, London
The Museum of Domestic Life, Great Yarmouth
Oxford City and County Museum, Woodstock, Oxford
City of Oxford Museum and Art Gallery, Oxford
Ryedale Folk Museum, Hutton-le-Hole, Yorkshire
National Museum of Antiquities of Scotland, Edinburgh
Museum of English Rural Life, Reading University

Index